My Emotions Journal.....

_____

_____

_____

_____

DATE:..........

Today I mostly feel........ (Circle one).

OR, you could...  Draw your OWN emoji?

Draw/ Stick/ Doodle About It!

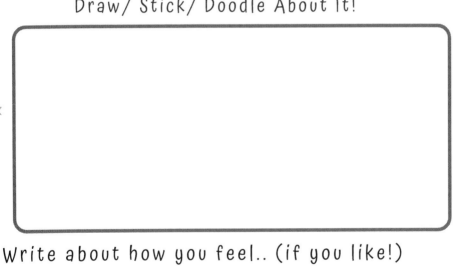

Write about how you feel.. (if you like!)

_____
_____
_____
_____
_____

Three Good Things About Today...

1)..

2)..

3)..

Something OR someone that helped me today was...

Something I would like to improve on tomorrow is...

Someone I can share my feelings with is ....

I could tell them by, drawing them a picture,
writing a note, or talking to them, (circle which!).

Dear _____

Today I Feel _____

_____

_____

Because _____

_____

_____

_____

(or Draw/doodle below!....)

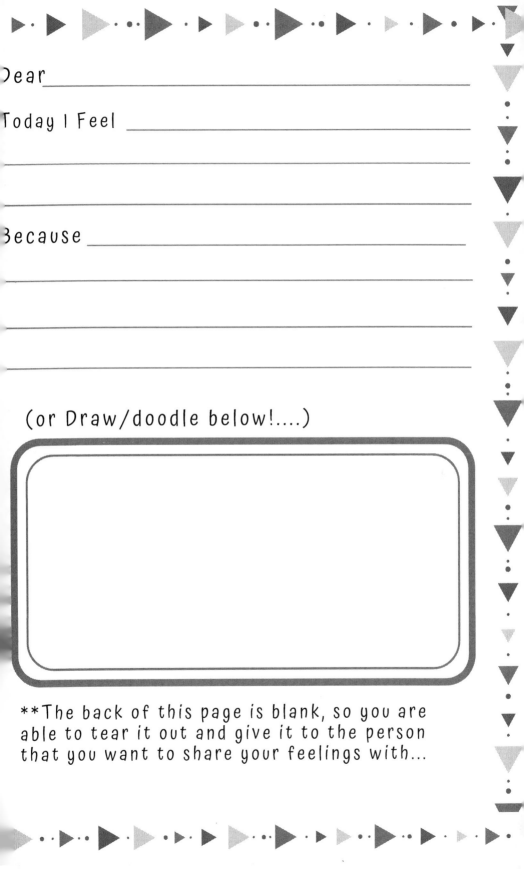

**The back of this page is blank, so you are able to tear it out and give it to the person that you want to share your feelings with...

DATE:..........

Today I mostly feel........ (Circle one).

OR, you could...   Draw your
                         OWN emoji?

Draw/ Stick/ Doodle About It!

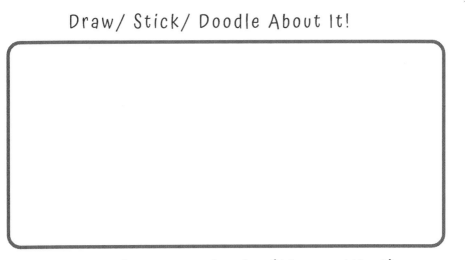

Write about how you feel.. (if you like!)

Three Good Things About Today...

1)..

2)..

3)..

Something OR someone that helped me today was...

Something I would like to improve on tomorrow is...

Someone I can share my feelings with is ....

I could tell them by, drawing them a picture,
writing a note, or talking to them, (circle which!).

Dear _____

Today I Feel _____

_____

_____

Because _____

_____

_____

_____

(or Draw/doodle below!....)

**The back of this page is blank, so you are able to tear it out and give it to the person that you want to share your feelings with...

DATE:..........

Today I mostly feel........ (Circle one).

OR, you could...   Draw your
OWN emoji?

Draw/ Stick/ Doodle About It!

Write about how you feel.. (if you like!)

Three Good Things About Today...

1)..

2)..

3)..

Something OR someone that helped me today was...

_____

_____

_____

Something I would like to improve on tomorrow is...

_____

_____

_____

Someone I can share my feelings with is ....

_____

_____

I could tell them by, drawing them a picture,
writing a note, or talking to them, (circle which!)

Dear _____

Today I Feel _____

_____

_____

Because _____

_____

_____

_____

(or Draw/doodle below!....)

**The back of this page is blank, so you are able to tear it out and give it to the person that you want to share your feelings with...

DATE:..........

Today I mostly feel........ (Circle one).

OR, you could...      Draw your
OWN emoji?

Draw/ Stick/ Doodle About It!

Write about how you feel.. (if you like!)

Three Good Things About Today...

1)...

2)...

3)...

Something OR someone that helped me today was...

Something I would like to improve on tomorrow is...

Someone I can share my feelings with is ....

I could tell them by, drawing them a picture,
writing a note, or talking to them, (circle which!)

Dear_____

Today I Feel _____

_____

_____

Because _____

_____

_____

_____

(or Draw/doodle below!....)

**The back of this page is blank, so you are able to tear it out and give it to the person that you want to share your feelings with...

DATE:..........

Today I mostly feel........ (Circle one).

OR, you could...   Draw your
                          OWN emoji?

Draw/ Stick/ Doodle About It!

Write about how you feel.. (if you like!)

Three Good Things About Today...

1)...

2)...

3)...

Something OR someone that helped me today was...

Something I would like to improve on tomorrow is...

Someone I can share my feelings with is ....

I could tell them by, drawing them a picture,
writing a note, or talking to them, (circle which!)

Dear _____

Today I Feel _____

_____

_____

Because _____

_____

_____

_____

(or Draw/doodle below!....)

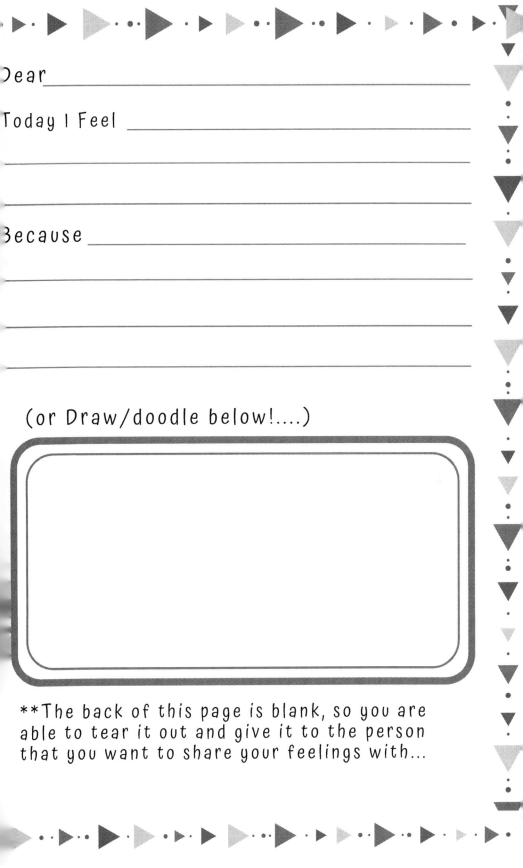

**The back of this page is blank, so you are able to tear it out and give it to the person that you want to share your feelings with...

DATE:..........

Today I mostly feel........ (Circle one).

OR, you could... Draw your OWN emoji?

Draw/ Stick/ Doodle About It!

Write about how you feel.. (if you like!)

_____

_____

_____

_____

Three Good Things About Today...

1)...

2)...

3)...

Something OR someone that helped me today was...

_____

_____

_____

_____

Something I would like to improve on tomorrow is...

_____

_____

_____

Someone I can share my feelings with is ....

_____

_____

I could tell them by, drawing them a picture, writing a note, or talking to them, (circle which!).

Dear_____

Today I Feel _____

_____

_____

Because _____

_____

_____

_____

(or Draw/doodle below!....)

**The back of this page is blank, so you are
able to tear it out and give it to the person
that you want to share your feelings with...

DATE:..........

Today I mostly feel........ (Circle one).

OR, you could... Draw your OWN emoji?

Draw/ Stick/ Doodle About It!

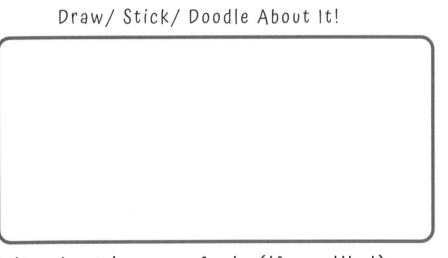

Write about how you feel.. (if you like!)

Three Good Things About Today...

1)...

2)...

3)...

Something OR someone that helped me today was...

Something I would like to improve on tomorrow is...

Someone I can share my feelings with is ....

I could tell them by, drawing them a picture,
writing a note, or talking to them, (circle which!).

Dear _____

Today I Feel _____

_____

Because _____

_____

_____

_____

(or Draw/doodle below!....)

**The back of this page is blank, so you are able to tear it out and give it to the person that you want to share your feelings with...

DATE:..........

Today I mostly feel........ (Circle one).

OR, you could... Draw your OWN emoji?

Draw/ Stick/ Doodle About It!

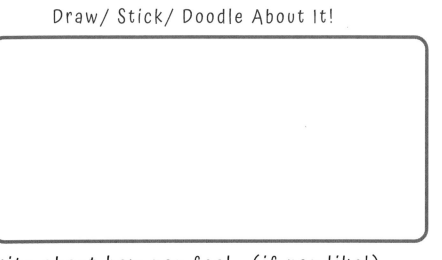

Write about how you feel.. (if you like!)

_____

_____

_____

_____

_____

Three Good Things About Today...

1)...

2)...

3)...

Something OR someone that helped me today was...

_____

_____

_____

Something I would like to improve on tomorrow is...

_____

_____

_____

Someone I can share my feelings with is ....

_____

_____

I could tell them by, drawing them a picture,
writing a note, or talking to them, (circle which!)

Dear _____

Today I Feel _____

_____

_____

Because _____

_____

_____

_____

(or Draw/doodle below!....)

**The back of this page is blank, so you are able to tear it out and give it to the person that you want to share your feelings with...

DATE:..........

Today I mostly feel........ (Circle one).

OR, you could... Draw your OWN emoji?

Draw/ Stick/ Doodle About It!

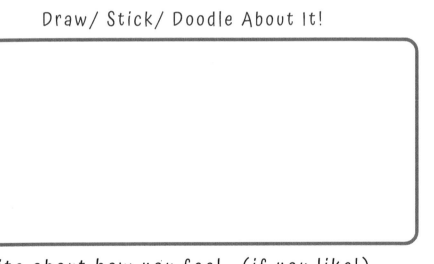

Write about how you feel.. (if you like!)

Three Good Things About Today...

1)...

2)...

3)...

Something OR someone that helped me today was...

Something I would like to improve on tomorrow is...

Someone I can share my feelings with is ....

I could tell them by, drawing them a picture, writing a note, or talking to them, (circle which!)

Dear _____

Today I Feel _____

_____

_____

Because _____

_____

_____

_____

(or Draw/doodle below!....)

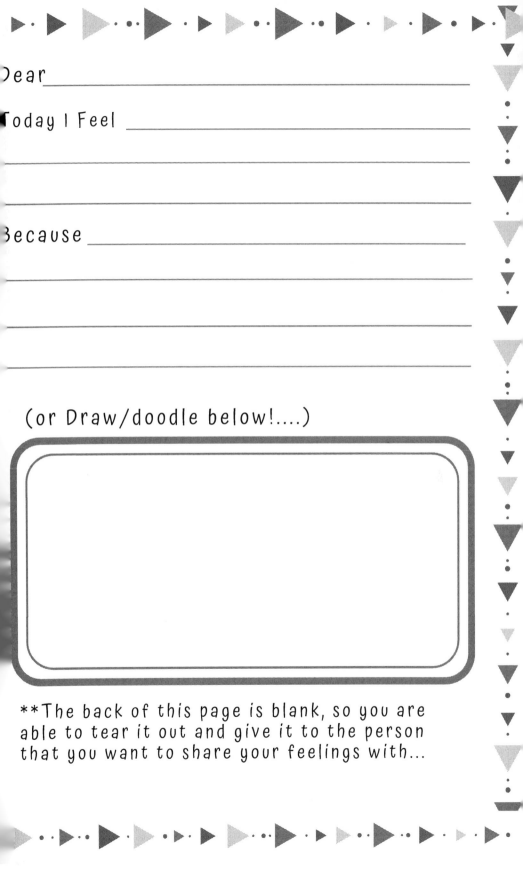

**The back of this page is blank, so you are able to tear it out and give it to the person that you want to share your feelings with...

DATE:..........

Today I mostly feel........ (Circle one).

OR, you could... Draw your OWN emoji?

Draw/ Stick/ Doodle About It!

Write about how you feel.. (if you like!)

_____

_____

_____

_____

Three Good Things About Today...

1)..

2)..

3)..

Something OR someone that helped me today was...

_____

_____

_____

_____

Something I would like to improve on tomorrow is...

_____

_____

_____

Someone I can share my feelings with is ....

_____

_____

I could tell them by, drawing them a picture,
writing a note, or talking to them, (circle which!)

Dear _____

Today I Feel _____

_____

_____

Because _____

_____

_____

_____

(or Draw/doodle below!....)

**The back of this page is blank, so you are able to tear it out and give it to the person that you want to share your feelings with...

DATE:..........

Today I mostly feel........ (Circle one).

OR, you could...  Draw your OWN emoji?

Draw/ Stick/ Doodle About It!

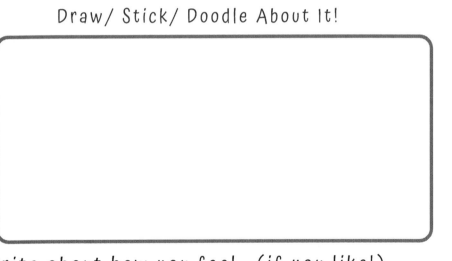

Write about how you feel.. (if you like!)

Three Good Things About Today...

1)...

2)...

3)...

Something OR someone that helped me today was...

_____

_____

_____

Something I would like to improve on tomorrow is...

_____

_____

_____

Someone I can share my feelings with is ....

_____

_____

I could tell them by, drawing them a picture, writing a note, or talking to them, (circle which!)

Dear _____

Today I Feel _____

_____

_____

Because _____

_____

_____

_____

(or Draw/doodle below!....)

**The back of this page is blank, so you are able to tear it out and give it to the person that you want to share your feelings with...

DATE:..........

Today I mostly feel........ (Circle one).

OR, you could... Draw your OWN emoji?

Draw/ Stick/ Doodle About It!

Write about how you feel.. (if you like!)

Three Good Things About Today...

1)...

2)...

3)...

Something OR someone that helped me today was...

Something I would like to improve on tomorrow is...

Someone I can share my feelings with is ....

I could tell them by, drawing them a picture,
writing a note, or talking to them, (circle which!)

Dear_____

Today I Feel _____

_____

Because _____

_____

_____

_____

(or Draw/doodle below!....)

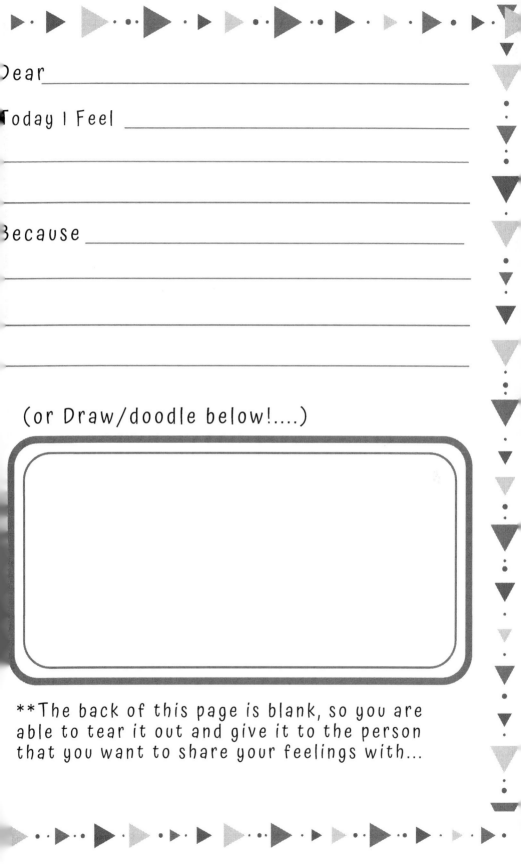

**The back of this page is blank, so you are able to tear it out and give it to the person that you want to share your feelings with...

DATE:..........

Today I mostly feel........ (Circle one).

OR, you could... Draw your OWN emoji?

Draw/ Stick/ Doodle About It!

Write about how you feel.. (if you like!)

Three Good Things About Today...

1)...

2)...

3)...

Something OR someone that helped me today was...

Something I would like to improve on tomorrow is...

Someone I can share my feelings with is ....

I could tell them by, drawing them a picture,
writing a note, or talking to them, (circle which!)

Dear _____

Today I Feel _____

_____

_____

Because _____

_____

_____

_____

(or Draw/doodle below!....)

**The back of this page is blank, so you are able to tear it out and give it to the person that you want to share your feelings with...

DATE:..........

Today I mostly feel........ (Circle one).

OR, you could...      Draw your
OWN emoji?

Draw/ Stick/ Doodle About It!

Write about how you feel.. (if you like!)

Three Good Things About Today...

1)...

2)...

3)...

Something OR someone that helped me today was...

Something I would like to improve on tomorrow is...

Someone I can share my feelings with is ....

I could tell them by, drawing them a picture, writing a note, or talking to them, (circle which!)

Dear _____

Today I Feel _____

_____

_____

Because _____

_____

_____

_____

(or Draw/doodle below!....)

**The back of this page is blank, so you are able to tear it out and give it to the person that you want to share your feelings with...

DATE:..........

Today I mostly feel........ (Circle one).

OR, you could...   Draw your
                                    OWN emoji?

Draw/ Stick/ Doodle About It!

Write about how you feel.. (if you like!)

Three Good Things About Today...

1)...

2)...

3)...

Something OR someone that helped me today was...

Something I would like to improve on tomorrow is...

Someone I can share my feelings with is ....

I could tell them by, drawing them a picture,
writing a note, or talking to them, (circle which!)

Dear _____

Today I Feel _____

_____

_____

Because _____

_____

_____

_____

(or Draw/doodle below!....)

**The back of this page is blank, so you are
able to tear it out and give it to the person
that you want to share your feelings with...

DATE:..........

Today I mostly feel........ (Circle one).

OR, you could...   Draw your
                          OWN emoji?

Draw/ Stick/ Doodle About It!

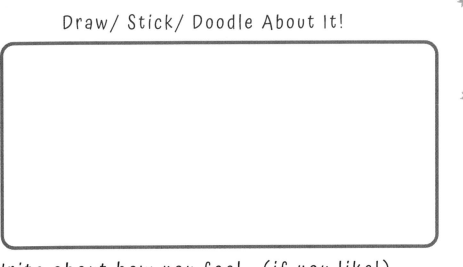

Write about how you feel.. (if you like!)

Three Good Things About Today...

1)..

2)..

3)..

Something OR someone that helped me today was...

Something I would like to improve on tomorrow is...

Someone I can share my feelings with is ....

I could tell them by, drawing them a picture,
writing a note, or talking to them, (circle which!)

ear _____

oday I Feel _____

_____

_____

ecause _____

_____

_____

_____

(or Draw/doodle below!....)

**The back of this page is blank, so you are able to tear it out and give it to the person that you want to share your feelings with...

DATE:..........

Today I mostly feel........ (Circle one).

OR, you could... Draw your OWN emoji?

Draw/ Stick/ Doodle About It!

Write about how you feel.. (if you like!)

Three Good Things About Today...

1) ....

2) ....

3) ....

Something OR someone that helped me today was...

_____

_____

_____

_____

Something I would like to improve on tomorrow is...

_____

_____

_____

Someone I can share my feelings with is ....

_____

_____

I could tell them by, drawing them a picture,
writing a note, or talking to them, (circle which!)

ear _____

oday I Feel _____

_____

_____

ecause _____

_____

_____

_____

(or Draw/doodle below!....)

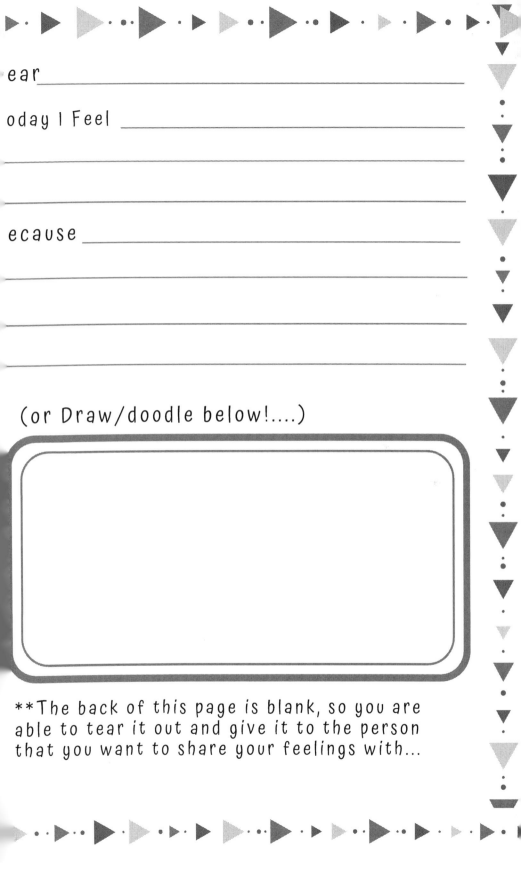

**The back of this page is blank, so you are
able to tear it out and give it to the person
that you want to share your feelings with...

DATE:..........

Today I mostly feel........ (Circle one).

OR, you could...   Draw your
                     OWN emoji?

Draw/ Stick/ Doodle About It!

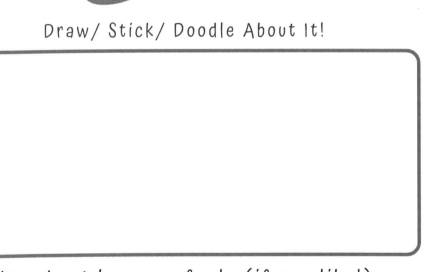

Write about how you feel.. (if you like!)

Three Good Things About Today...

1) ....

2) ....

3) ....

Something OR someone that helped me today was...

_____

_____

_____

_____

Something I would like to improve on tomorrow is...

_____

_____

_____

_____

Someone I can share my feelings with is ....

_____

_____

I could tell them by, drawing them a picture,
writing a note, or talking to them, (circle which!)

ear_____

oday I Feel _____

_____

_____

ecause _____

_____

_____

_____

(or Draw/doodle below!....)

**The back of this page is blank, so you are able to tear it out and give it to the person that you want to share your feelings with...

DATE:..........

Today I mostly feel........ (Circle one).

OR, you could...  Draw your OWN emoji?

Draw/ Stick/ Doodle About It!

Write about how you feel.. (if you like!)

Three Good Things About Today...

1) ....

2) ....

3) ....

Something OR someone that helped me today was...

_____

_____

_____

_____

Something I would like to improve on tomorrow is...

_____

_____

_____

_____

Someone I can share my feelings with is ....

_____

_____

I could tell them by, drawing them a picture,
writing a note, or talking to them, (circle which!)

ear_____

oday I Feel _____

_____

_____

ecause _____

_____

_____

_____

(or Draw/doodle below!....)

**The back of this page is blank, so you are able to tear it out and give it to the person that you want to share your feelings with...

DATE:..........

Today I mostly feel........ (Circle one).

OR, you could...   Draw your
                        OWN emoji?

Draw/ Stick/ Doodle About It!

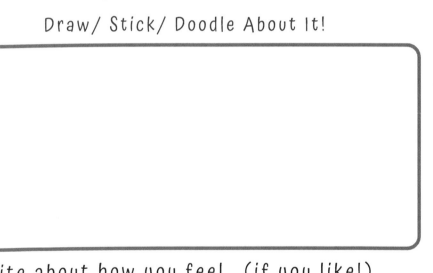

Write about how you feel.. (if you like!)

Three Good Things About Today...

1)...

2)...

3)...

Something OR someone that helped me today was...

_____

_____

_____

_____

Something I would like to improve on tomorrow is...

_____

_____

_____

_____

Someone I can share my feelings with is ....

_____

_____

I could tell them by, drawing them a picture,
writing a note, or talking to them, (circle which!)

ear _____

oday I Feel _____

_____

_____

ecause _____

_____

_____

_____

(or Draw/doodle below!....)

**The back of this page is blank, so you are
able to tear it out and give it to the person
that you want to share your feelings with...

DATE:..........

Today I mostly feel........ (Circle one).

OR, you could...   Draw your
                        OWN emoji?

Draw/ Stick/ Doodle About It!

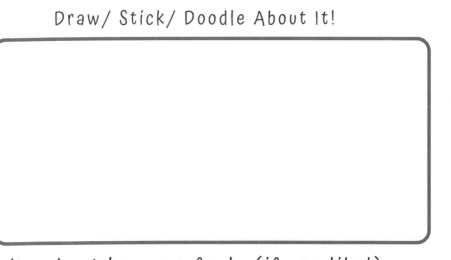

Write about how you feel.. (if you like!)

Three Good Things About Today...

1)..

2)..

3)..

Something OR someone that helped me today was...

Something I would like to improve on tomorrow is...

Someone I can share my feelings with is ....

I could tell them by, drawing them a picture,
writing a note, or talking to them, (circle which!)

ear_____

oday I Feel _____

_____

_____

ecause _____

_____

_____

_____

(or Draw/doodle below!....)

**The back of this page is blank, so you are able to tear it out and give it to the person that you want to share your feelings with...

DATE:..........

Today I mostly feel........ (Circle one).

OR, you could...   Draw your
                   OWN emoji?

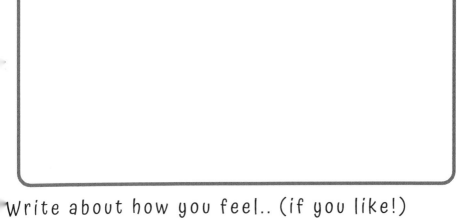

Draw/ Stick/ Doodle About It!

Write about how you feel.. (if you like!)

Three Good Things About Today...

1)...

2)...

3)...

Something OR someone that helped me today was...

Something I would like to improve on tomorrow is...

Someone I can share my feelings with is ....

I could tell them by, drawing them a picture,
writing a note, or talking to them, (circle which!)

ear_____

oday I Feel _____

_____

_____

ecause _____

_____

_____

_____

(or Draw/doodle below!....)

**The back of this page is blank, so you are able to tear it out and give it to the person that you want to share your feelings with...

DATE:..........

Today I mostly feel........ (Circle one).

OR, you could...  Draw your
OWN emoji?

Draw/ Stick/ Doodle About It!

Write about how you feel.. (if you like!)

Three Good Things About Today...

1)...

2)...

3)...

Something OR someone that helped me today was...

_____

_____

_____

_____

Something I would like to improve on tomorrow is...

_____

_____

_____

Someone I can share my feelings with is ....

_____

_____

I could tell them by, drawing them a picture, writing a note, or talking to them, (circle which!)

ear_____

oday I Feel _____

_____

_____

ecause _____

_____

_____

_____

(or Draw/doodle below!....)

**The back of this page is blank, so you are able to tear it out and give it to the person that you want to share your feelings with...

DATE:..........

Today I mostly feel........ (Circle one).

OR, you could...   Draw your
                          OWN emoji?

Draw/ Stick/ Doodle About It!

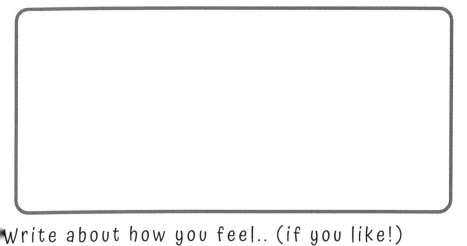

Write about how you feel.. (if you like!)

Three Good Things About Today...

1)...

2)...

3)...

Something OR someone that helped me today was...

Something I would like to improve on tomorrow is...

Someone I can share my feelings with is ....

I could tell them by, drawing them a picture,
writing a note, or talking to them, (circle which!)

ear_____

oday I Feel _____

_____

_____

ecause _____

_____

_____

_____

(or Draw/doodle below!....)

**The back of this page is blank, so you are able to tear it out and give it to the person that you want to share your feelings with...

DATE:...........

Today I mostly feel........ (Circle one).

OR, you could... Draw your OWN emoji?

Draw/ Stick/ Doodle About It!

Write about how you feel.. (if you like!)

_____

_____

_____

_____

_____

Three Good Things About Today...

1)...

2)...

3)...

Something OR someone that helped me today was...

_____

_____

_____

_____

Something I would like to improve on tomorrow is...

_____

_____

_____

Someone I can share my feelings with is ....

_____

_____

I could tell them by, drawing them a picture,
writing a note, or talking to them, (circle which!)

ear _____

oday I Feel _____

_____

_____

ecause _____

_____

_____

_____

(or Draw/doodle below!....)

**The back of this page is blank, so you are able to tear it out and give it to the person that you want to share your feelings with...

DATE:.........

Today I mostly feel........ (Circle one).

OR, you could...  Draw your
OWN emoji?

Draw/ Stick/ Doodle About It!

Write about how you feel.. (if you like!)

Three Good Things About Today...

1)...

2)...

3)...

Something OR someone that helped me today was...

_____

_____

_____

_____

Something I would like to improve on tomorrow is...

_____

_____

_____

Someone I can share my feelings with is ....

_____

_____

I could tell them by, drawing them a picture, writing a note, or talking to them, (circle which!)

ear_____

oday I Feel _____

_____

_____

ecause _____

_____

_____

_____

(or Draw/doodle below!....)

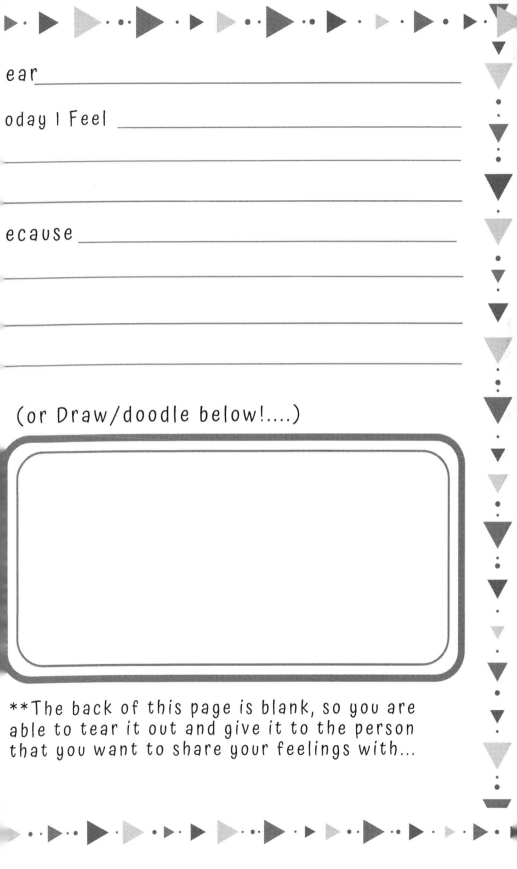

**The back of this page is blank, so you are able to tear it out and give it to the person that you want to share your feelings with...

DATE:...........

Today I mostly feel........ (Circle one).

OR, you could...   Draw your
                         OWN emoji?

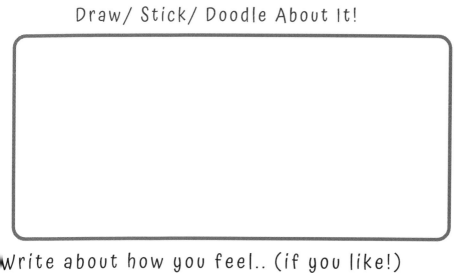

Draw/ Stick/ Doodle About It!

Write about how you feel.. (if you like!)

_____

_____

_____

_____

_____

Three Good Things About Today...

1).....................................

2).....................................

3).....................................

Something OR someone that helped me today was...

Something I would like to improve on tomorrow is...

Someone I can share my feelings with is ....

I could tell them by, drawing them a picture,
writing a note, or talking to them, (circle which!)

ear_____

oday I Feel _____

_____

_____

ecause _____

_____

_____

_____

(or Draw/doodle below!....)

**The back of this page is blank, so you are able to tear it out and give it to the person that you want to share your feelings with...

DATE:..........

Today I mostly feel........ (Circle one).

OR, you could...   Draw your
                         OWN emoji?

Draw/ Stick/ Doodle About It!

Write about how you feel.. (if you like!)

Three Good Things About Today...

1)...

2)...

3)...

Something OR someone that helped me today was...

Something I would like to improve on tomorrow is..

Someone I can share my feelings with is ....

I could tell them by, drawing them a picture,
writing a note, or talking to them, (circle which!)

ear_____

oday I Feel _____

_____

_____

ecause _____

_____

_____

_____

(or Draw/doodle below!....)

**The back of this page is blank, so you are
able to tear it out and give it to the person
that you want to share your feelings with...

DATE:..........

Today I mostly feel........ (Circle one).

OR, you could...   Draw your
                        OWN emoji?

Draw/ Stick/ Doodle About It!

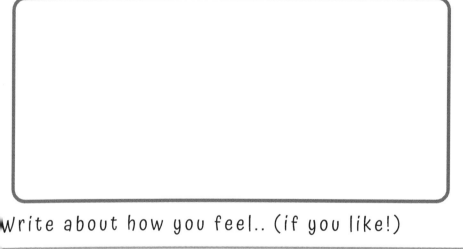

Write about how you feel.. (if you like!)

_____

_____

_____

_____

_____

Three Good Things About Today...

1)...

2)...

3)...

Something OR someone that helped me today was..

Something I would like to improve on tomorrow is..

Someone I can share my feelings with is ....

I could tell them by, drawing them a picture,
writing a note, or talking to them, (circle which!)

ear _____

oday I Feel _____

_____

_____

ecause _____

_____

_____

_____

(or Draw/doodle below!....)

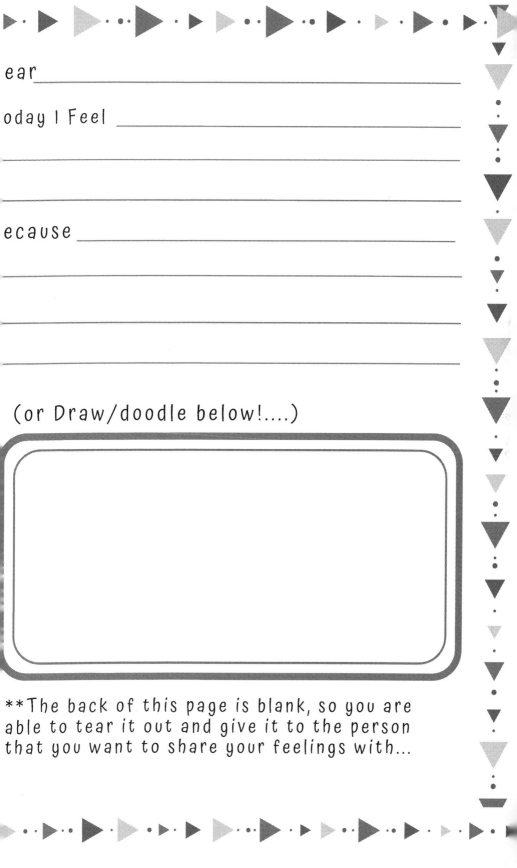

**The back of this page is blank, so you are able to tear it out and give it to the person that you want to share your feelings with...

DATE:..........

Today I mostly feel........ (Circle one).

OR, you could...   Draw your
OWN emoji?

Draw/ Stick/ Doodle About It!

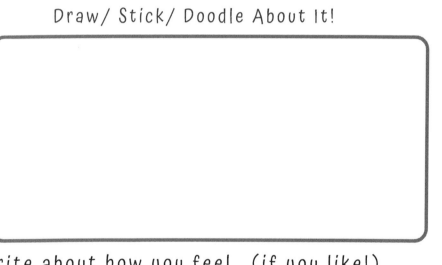

Write about how you feel.. (if you like!)

_____

_____

_____

_____

_____

Three Good Things About Today...

1)...

2)...

3)...

Something OR someone that helped me today was..

Something I would like to improve on tomorrow is..

Someone I can share my feelings with is ....

I could tell them by, drawing them a picture,
writing a note, or talking to them, (circle which!)

ear_____

oday I Feel _____

_____

_____

ecause _____

_____

_____

_____

(or Draw/doodle below!....)

**The back of this page is blank, so you are able to tear it out and give it to the person that you want to share your feelings with...

Made in the USA
Las Vegas, NV
21 January 2024

84724381R00070